BLUE BANNER BIOGRAPHY

LL Cool J

Tammy Gagne

Mitchell Lane
PUBLISHERS
P.O. Box 196
Hockessin, Delaware 19707
Visit us on the web: www.mitchelllane.com
Comments? Email us: mitchelllane@mitchelllane.com

Mitchell Lane
PUBLISHERS

Printing   1   2   3   4   5   6   7   8   9

Blue Banner Biographies

Abby Wambach	Ice Cube	Miguel Tejada
Adele	Ja Rule	Mike Trout
Alicia Keys	Jamie Foxx	Nancy Pelosi
Allen Iverson	Jay-Z	Natasha Bedingfield
Ashanti	Jennifer Hudson	Nicki Minaj
Ashlee Simpson	Jennifer Lopez	One Direction
Ashton Kutcher	Jessica Simpson	Orianthi
Avril Lavigne	J. K. Rowling	Orlando Bloom
Blake Lively	John Legend	P. Diddy
Bow Wow	Justin Berfield	Peyton Manning
Brett Favre	Justin Timberlake	Prince William
Britney Spears	Kanye West	Queen Latifah
Bruno Mars	Kate Hudson	Robert Downey Jr.
CC Sabathia	Katy Perry	Ron Howard
Carrie Underwood	Keith Urban	Sean Kingston
Chris Brown	Kelly Clarkson	Shakira
Chris Daughtry	Kenny Chesney	Shia LaBeouf
Christina Aguilera	Ke$ha	Shontelle Layne
Clay Aiken	Kevin Durant	Soulja Boy Tell 'Em
Cole Hamels	Kristen Stewart	Stephenie Meyer
Condoleezza Rice	Lady Gaga	Taylor Swift
Corbin Bleu	Lance Armstrong	T.I.
Daniel Radcliffe	Leona Lewis	Timbaland
David Ortiz	Lionel Messi	Tim McGraw
David Wright	Lindsay Lohan	Tim Tebow
Derek Jeter	**LL Cool J**	Toby Keith
Drew Brees	Ludacris	Usher
Eminem	Mariah Carey	Vanessa Anne Hudgens
Eve	Mario	Will.i.am
Fergie	Mary J. Blige	Zac Efron
Flo Rida	Mary-Kate and Ashley Olsen	
Gwen Stefani	Megan Fox	

Library of Congress Cataloging-in-Publication Data
Gagne, Tammy.
LL Cool J / by Tammy Gagne.
    pages cm
Includes bibliographical references and index.
ISBN 978-1-61228-464-4 (library bound)
1. LL Cool J, 1968– —Juvenile literature. 2. Rap musicians—United States—Biography—Juvenile literature. I. Title.
ML3930.L115G34 2013
782.421649092—dc23
[B]
                                                                                                          2013023039
eBook ISBN: 9781612285214

ABOUT THE AUTHOR: Tammy Gagne is the author of numerous books for adults and children, including *Ke$ha* and *Will.i.am* for Mitchell Lane Publishers. She resides in northern New England with her husband and son. One of her favorite pastimes is visiting schools to speak to kids about the writing process.

PUBLISHER'S NOTE: The following story has been thoroughly researched, and to the best of our knowledge represents a true story. While every possible effort has been made to ensure accuracy, the publisher will not assume liability for damages caused by inaccuracies in the data and makes no warranty on the accuracy of the information contained herein. This story has not been authorized or endorsed by LL Cool J.

Blue Banner Biography

LL Cool J plays Special Agent Sam Hanna on CBS's hit television show NCIS: Los Angeles. Acting is just one of the jobs that LL has done since entering show business. He has also been a successful rap artist for nearly 30 years.

A Rough Start

*T*une in to *NCIS: Los Angeles* any Tuesday night, and you will see LL Cool J playing Special Agent Sam Hanna. You can also hear this multitalented star singing his many hit rap songs on any of his 13 albums. How does a performer rise to fame in 1985 and remain just as popular now as he was back then? "I'm not afraid to change and grow," he told *Ebony* magazine. "Music is just a part of my life, a consistent part of my life that is important to me. It's always a challenge coming up with new ideas, but I love it. It's just what I do. It's like playing sports. You're in the zone and you just go for it. Love makes it much easier. And I love what I do."

LL Cool J was born James Todd Smith in St. Albans, a district in New York City, on January 14, 1968. His first name never really stuck, though. Although a few strict teachers insisted on calling him James, no one outside of school used it. As he explained to *Long Island Pulse Magazine* in 2010, "LL is my performing name, the one that I use publicly. Privately, a lot of people call me Todd. It's never been James."

Todd started calling himself LL Cool J when he was just 14. It stands for "Ladies Love Cool James." At the time, he thought it would be a good stage name for a rap artist. He was right. More than 30 years later, the ladies indeed adore him, and the men think he's pretty cool, too.

Todd's early years weren't easy. After years of abuse, his mother Ondrea Smith decided to leave his father, James Nunya, when Todd was four years old. She and Todd moved in with her parents. Todd's father wanted his wife to come back. When she refused, he arrived one day with a shotgun and shot both her and Todd's grandfather, Eugene.

Miraculously, both Ondrea and her father survived. LL told *Jet* magazine, "The way my family handled that incident—no charges pressed, that forgiveness—showed love in a way I have never seen since. From the way my family dealt with the shooting, I learned forgiveness and

LL Cool J and his mother, Ondrea Smith

gained inner strength. That lesson helped me become who I am today."

Unfortunately, the rough times weren't over for young Todd. While Ondrea was recovering, she met a physical therapist named Roscoe. On the surface he seemed caring and supportive. To Todd, though, his mother's new boyfriend was physically and verbally abusive. In his 1997 book, *I Make My Own Rules*, LL describes how Roscoe beat him with his fists and with household objects like extension cords and vacuum cleaner attachments. "Living with Roscoe was like being a little kid who gets to play in the daisy field every day," he wrote. "But every evening that kid has to go home and sleep in a cemetery with a dragon. It was the most horrible experience. I was defenseless and I didn't understand. The pain went so deep."

"Living with Roscoe was like being a little kid who gets to play in the daisy field every day," he wrote. "But every evening that kid has to go home and sleep in a cemetery with a dragon."

He turned to rap music to help him

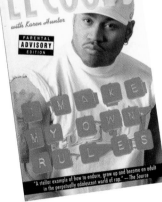

THE NATIONAL BESTSELLER
LL COOL J
with Karen Hunter
PARENTAL ADVISORY EDITION
I MAKE MY OWN RULES
"A stellar example of how to endure, grow up and become an adult in the perpetually adolescent world of rap." — The Source

through this difficult time. As he told *Jet*, "The music and rhymes helped me escape all the pain. I couldn't have cared less about the cars, the clothes . . . What [rappers] had that I wanted most was the power to say whatever they wanted."

Todd had loved rap music from the time he was a young boy. He told the *New York Times*, "In this neighborhood, the kids grow up in rap. It's like speaking Spanish if you grow up in an all-Spanish house. I got into it when I was about 9, and since then all I wanted was to make a record and hear it on the radio."

Todd's grandfather helped him move toward that goal. Eugene bought his grandson his first mixing table when he was just 11. "I think he did it to keep me out of trouble," LL told *Long Island Pulse Magazine*, "to keep me in the house and to help me do what I seemed to be passionate about."

Todd put the gift to good use right away. He began writing lyrics and performing songs of his own. He rapped with several groups in his neighborhood. They would appear at block parties and roller rinks.

LL remembers how they would entertain the crowd and dare each other at the same time. He explained to the *New York Times*, "Aspiring rappers like to challenge each other with disrespect. They come up to each other and accuse each other of being washed-up winos, anything insulting. Or it's Friday night at the roller rink and a rapper announces, 'I can take out any rapper with just one rhyme.' Somebody else says, 'Man, you can't take nobody out with one rhyme.' And it starts from there. Being the best in your neighborhood is what it's all about."

> *"Aspiring rappers like to challenge each other with disrespect. . . . 'Man, you can't take nobody out with one rhyme.' And it starts from there. Being the best in your neighborhood is what it's all about."*

Fighting His Way to the Top

*T*odd spent a lot of time with his grandparents while he was in junior high school. They were positive role models for the young boy, the victim of a horrible bully at home. Unfortunately, like many victims of bullies, LL became a bully himself. "I couldn't fight back in my house; I was defenseless there," LL wrote in his book. "But on the streets I wasn't going to let anybody else beat me, not without a good fight."

When LL was 13, he started sending tapes of his songs out to record labels that worked with rap artists. None showed any interest. When he was 16, however, he sent a tape to Rick Rubin, a New York University student. Rubin and his partner Russell Simmons were starting their own label, Def Jam. They liked LL's sound and decided to sign him. LL's song "I Need a Beat" became Def Jam's first single in 1984. It sold more than 100,000 copies.

When "I Need a Beat" took off, LL decided to drop out of Andrew Jackson High School to focus on his rap music career. It was the first in a series of bad choices he would make. He also got involved with drugs and alcohol.

LL Cool J signed with Def Jam Recordings in 1984. He remained with the label until 2008 when he released his 12th album, Exit 13. *It wouldn't be his last album, though. He released* Authentic *in 2013 with S-BRO Music Group.*

Ondrea eventually left Roscoe. "You know how glad I was to have Roscoe out of my life," LL shared, "but the damage was done. I was doing all kinds of wild things by then and getting in all kinds of trouble."

Today he says he is thankful that his bad decisions didn't end up killing him. "It wasn't easy to get back in control," he told *Jet* magazine. "Somehow I overcame the drugs and the alcohol. But I needed help. I needed strength. I had to dig deep down inside myself and find who I really was, and force myself to understand what I saw."

Despite his challenges, LL's career took off. His first album, *Radio*, was released in 1985 and went platinum with more than 1,500,000 sales. He performed "I Can't Live

LL Cool J and his wife Simone attend the CNN Heroes Event in Los Angeles, California in 2010. The celebration honors everyday heroes doing extraordinary work. LL was one of the presenters at the show.

Without My Radio" in the 1985 film *Krush Groove*, in which he had a small role. The following year he briefly appeared in the film *Wildcats*. He also wrote and performed the movie's theme song.

He released his second album, *Bigger and Deffer*, in 1987. The song "I'm Bad" made it to number 4 on the R&B chart, and the album itself went double platinum. That means it sold more than 2,000,000 copies. Another song, the ballad "I Need Love," reached number 14 on the pop chart and turned LL into a crossover artist. He was blazing a trail for other rap artists, bringing the rap sound to mainstream music.

It was around this time that he met Simone Johnson, his future wife. "It was Easter, and I was driving down the block in my mother's car," LL told Jimmy Kimmel on *Jimmy Kimmel Live* in 2012. He had stopped the car to say hello to a friend when the friend asked LL if he wanted to meet his cousin. LL almost said no, but then he saw her. "I looked over and said 'Oh yeah, I'll meet your cousin.'"

He and Simone dated on and off over the next several years. LL hadn't given up his party lifestyle at this point, though. He told *Jet* magazine, "I feel really blessed that Simone waited for me to grow up. I'm glad she endured and stuck by me during the rough times."

LL recorded the song "Goin' Back to Cali" for the *Less Than Zero* soundtrack in 1988. It too did well on both the pop and R&B charts. That year he also headlined the Def Jam tour and played an anti-drug concert for the Just Say No Foundation at Radio City Music Hall.

In 1989, he released his third album, *Walking With a Panther*. This CD produced another crossover hit, "I'm That Type of Guy." The album made it to number 6 on the pop chart and number 1 on the R&B chart, but it wasn't very popular with many of his rap fans. They thought LL was trying to sound too much like a pop artist.

> *"I feel really blessed that Simone waited for me to grow up. I'm glad she endured and stuck by me during the rough times."*

A Time to Act

*L*L regained the respect from his early fans when he released the album *Mama Said Knock You Out* in 1990. It earned LL a Grammy and became his best-selling album of all time.

His increasing fame was helping LL tear down even more walls for rap artists. In 1991, he became the first rap artist to appear on MTV's *Unplugged*. His performance received rave reviews. Many people hoped he would return for a second appearance, but he never did. He explained to *Rolling Stone*, "Sometimes when you have a great moment, you just have to let it be that. I don't know about trying to recapture it. It was just one of those things that happened, and it was real honest and real natural, and I didn't think it out. If I did it now, I might be thinking, and that might be a problem. Instead of coming off cool, it might come off like, 'Oh, LL's trying to do that *Unplugged* thing again, and it's not as cool as before.'"

Trying to stay cool proved to be LL's downfall on his next album, 1993's *14 Shots to the Dome*. Many listeners thought the album was too heavy on West Coast gangsta

LL Cool J performed "Mama Said Knock You Out" at the Keep Memory Alive foundation's Power of Love gala at the MGM Grand Garden Arena in Las Vegas, Nevada in 2012. The event, which celebrated Muhammad Ali's 70th birthday, raised money for the Cleveland Clinic Lou Ruvo Center for Brain Health and the Muhammad Ali Center.

rap. Others felt it simply didn't offer anything new. *Rolling Stone* called it "Mama Said, Part II." The *Village Voice* picked the CD as its Dud of the Month, stating that LL couldn't "figure out how to mix rap and success." Unlike his previous albums, it only went gold (sales between 500,000 and 1,000,000). None of its four singles made the Top 20.

> The *Village Voice picked the CD as its Dud of the Month, stating that LL couldn't "figure out how to mix rap and success."*

By now, LL had begun to branch out. He had been given a couple of small film roles in the past. Now he wanted to do more than just dabble in acting. He played a detective in the action/comedy *The Hard Way* in 1991. The next year he was a former special forces soldier in the fantasy/comedy *Toys*. Neither movie was a huge success, but they did lead to his first starring role on the big screen, the 1995 crime drama called *Out-of-Sync*. The film didn't get great reviews, but people definitely talked about it. It was the first time LL had appeared without a hat. Whether on stage or in a film, he had always worn one. He is said to own more than 2,000 hats.

In 1995, he also began starring in his own television comedy series, *In the House*, playing former football player Marion Hill. Hill has to rent rooms in his house to pay his bills. It ran for two seasons on NBC and three more on UPN.

For a while now, LL had also been known by another name: Dad. While he was building his career, he and Simone were building something even more important, a

LL and his wife Simone visit Cirque Du Soleil's "Wintuk" at WaMu Theater at New York's Madison Square Garden in 2008 with their children.

family. Their son Najee was born in 1989. Daughters Italia and Samaria came along in 1991 and 1995. A third daughter, Nina, would be born in 2000.

LL continued to record his music while working on *In the House*. His 1995 album *Mr. Smith* went multiplatinum. Three songs from the album made it into the Top 10. He followed these hits up with three more off his next album, *Phenomenon*, in 1997. He also wrote his autobiography, *I Make My Own Rules*.

When *In the House* was cancelled, LL decided to pursue more serious acting roles. He wanted to play a drug lord in the crime thriller *In Too Deep*, but he was going to have to work for it. The producers worried that LL was too likable to play a bad guy. "I had to fight for the role, because of the image that was created by the other films I've done so far," he told the *Pittsburgh Post* shortly after the film's release in 1999. "I had to jump through a lot of hoops to convince the director I was capable of being menacing, being a villain."

> *"You shouldn't limit yourself. I think I have more stories to tell in acting than rapping right now . . . Because you know what—it's so refreshing to be new at something again."*

Although the movie got mixed reviews, many critics praised LL's performance. He went on to appear alongside some of the biggest stars in the movie industry in such films as *Any Given Sunday* (1999), *Deep Blue Sea* (1999), and *S.W.A.T.* in 2003. He was also becoming a pretty big star in his own right.

Between these films, he served as the co-host of the 2001 American Music Awards. Again, the reviews were good. The audience really seemed to enjoy his style and wit.

What LL seemed to enjoy most, though, was acting. "I think the best thing rap music has done for me is give me the opportunity to do a lot of different things," he told the *Pittsburgh Post*. "You shouldn't limit yourself. I think I have more stories to tell in acting than rapping right now. . . . Because you know what— it's so refreshing to be new at something again."

Putting It All Together

*L*L had finally done what some of his critics insisted he couldn't: balancing his success with rap. He released three albums between 2000 and 2004—*G.O.A.T.*, *10*, and *The DEFinition*. G.O.A.T. stood for the "greatest of all time." This title reminded many people of legendary boxer Muhammad Ali, known by that nickname for decades. Like Ali, LL is both self-assured and charming—which can be a difficult balance for many people in the spotlight.

When a reporter from the *Atlanta Journal* asked him if he still thought he was the greatest of all time in 2008, he answered, "Of course." She probably expected the same response when she asked if his answer applied to acting as well. But he immediately turned humble. "I think I'm still growing. I think I'm still growing in both areas. You're always learning. You're never, like, finished," he declared.

LL seemed to be doing a little of everything. He appeared in the Fox television medical drama *House* in 2005. In 2006, he played the love interest of Queen Latifah's character in the film *Last Holiday*. He recorded an episode of the NBC comedy *30 Rock* the following year. He was

LL hosted the 55th Annual Grammy Awards at the Staples Center in Los Angeles, California in 2013. He also closed the show by performing "Whaddup" and "Rock the Bells."

showing the world that he was capable of both serious roles and being funny. He also released another album in 2006, the self-titled CD called *Todd Smith*.

LL began using his real name for other professional pursuits that year. One project was a clothing line called Todd Smith. He described it to *Newsday* as a pure luxury brand: "The thing that separates it from the other brands out there is that the line is classy, it draws from classic tailoring—as opposed to your crotch being down to your ankles, or your shirt being oversized. It fits a person the way a garment is supposed to fit. Your size is your size."

Using his name for the line was important. "I want people to know that LL Cool J is more than just a rapper, and that there is a real human being behind it. With all the things associated with rap nowadays, it's important to me that people know that I'm a guy who loves his family, a guy that believes in God, a guy that has values." It was easy to see that LL had come a long way from his early days.

Yet another sign of LL's changes was his muscular physique. For some time the press had been asking him about his fitness routine almost as much as his music and acting. In 2007, he answered the question of how he stayed in such great shape by writing a book called *LL Cool J's Platinum Workout*. He explained to BodyBuilder. com that he hadn't always looked or felt the way he wanted. "I wrote this book for several reasons. I pride myself in taking care of my body. In 2002 I was preparing to tour for my latest album and I knew that if I wanted to be the best I could be on stage, I needed to get in better physical shape. It wasn't all about physical appearances. I wasn't happy with how I felt either. It's not that I was ever obese, but I also didn't take the time for me and I could see it physically and feel it."

The book offers detailed instructions for working out and eating right. LL knows that both exercise and food play important roles in good health. He stresses that the key to a balanced diet is eating the right amounts of everything. "If I didn't enjoy some treats in moderation, I wouldn't be a happy camper," he explains in the book. "You just have to

LL Cool J posed in clothes from his Todd Smith clothing line at the Regatta USA booth at the MAGIC Convention in Las Vegas, Nevada in 2008. The line features high-end, classically tailored clothing that fits the body like clothing should.

know how to control what you eat and make those smart choices most of the time. I absolutely enjoy desserts and other foods like that, some of the time."

In 2008, LL decided to start a second clothing line. This time he partnered with Sears to develop the LL Cool J Collection of affordable apparel. The Todd Smith line was being sold at high-end boutiques, but this brand would be more reasonably priced for everyday people. Sears also had a special place in LL's heart.

He shared his hopes for the line with *Brandweek* magazine. "I see the LL Cool J brand bringing families closer together. It was a priority for me to launch with a partner who connects with all of America and Sears does it best. One of the happiest times I can remember was my grandfather taking me to Sears every weekend when I was a child."

Unfortunately, he launched the new line just as the country was entering a recession. Even though Sears invested millions of dollars in promotions, the collection didn't sell very well and it was discontinued in 2009.

> *"I see the LL Cool J brand bringing families closer together. It was a priority for me to launch with a partner who connects with all of America and Sears does it best."*

Goin' Back to Cali

*A*much happier event that year was the television role that seemed to be made just for him: Special Agent Sam Hanna on *NCIS: Los Angeles*. It was a spinoff of the popular CBS crime drama *NCIS*. LL's character is a former Navy SEAL who served in Afghanistan, Bosnia, and Iraq. He is now a member of the Naval Criminal Investigative Service.

LL told *Long Island Pulse Magazine*, "I had never watched the show prior to hearing about the spin-off idea, so I went back and watched it, watched a marathon of the show, over and over and over again. And I realized that I could relate to it, that the show is fun and full of wit and humor. I like the banter. I think the stories are really cool and the chemistry is really great."

He was eager to be part of the project. "It's really exciting for me to finally be doing something where I'm actually, like, new," he told the *Chicago Tribune*. "I'm not like the elder statesman of hip-hop walking into the room. I'm actually like an unproven guy that's trying to make something happen for you guys, and that's a great dynamic

When LL Cool J hosted the 2012 Grammy Awards, he began the show with a prayer for the late Whitney Houston, who passed away just 24 hours earlier. It was an emotional night filled with both sadness over Houston's death and celebration of music.

for me. . . . This is not LL Cool J solo on the microphone, you know, ripping his tank top off."

LL was also excited about reaching a new audience. "I'm not interested in pretending that I'm 19, spending the rest of my life repeating myself on the radio talking about my new single," he told the *New York Post*. "It's a lot of fun to just do something new and reach some new people in Idaho, Kansas, Montana—touch some new worlds."

> **"It's a lot of fun to just do something new and reach some new people in Idaho, Kansas, Montana—touch some new worlds."**

He didn't worry that being part of the show would take him away from his younger audience. "As a guy that was born and raised in New York City," he told the *Post*, "I can tell you that there's a lot of cool things happening and hopefully the kids will be able to relate to it."

His music may even bring some rap fans to the show. LL wrote a song about his love for the show called "NCIS: No Crew Is Superior." He also released another album in 2008, titled *Exit 13*. It would be his last CD for Def Jam Recordings, not his last album. *Authentic* was released in 2013.

Music will always be a part of LL Cool J's life. The Grammy Awards asked him to host their annual awards ceremony in 2012. The 2012 audience liked him so much that he was invited back in 2013.

With all that he has accomplished in his career, though, LL seems most proud of his family. He credits his wife and children with making him the man he is today. He told *Ebony* magazine, "I'm more of a laid-back kind of father.

Fatherhood is an opportunity to set an example. It's an opportunity to prepare somebody to go out into the world and make a difference in a positive way. Being a father is a beautiful part of my life."

Oprah Winfrey visited LL and his family at their home in Los Angeles for an interview in 2013 and asked his children to finish the sentence, "The best thing your father ever taught you was—" His son Najee replied, "You can do anything you want if you put your mind to it. Just stay focused."

He wants to teach his kids how important they are. "Knowing your value is very important," he told *Jet* magazine. "I don't mean just value as a commodity-type value but knowing your value as a human being."

LL sees the value in the life lessons he has learned. "There's always things that you think you could have done differently, but . . . if you get on a chessboard, a mistake could turn out to be the thing that leads to your greatest success. So sometimes the things that you think were bad for you, might have ultimately helped you."

He is living proof of the truth of that belief. LL's road hasn't been an easy one, but his determination has definitely paid off. After nearly three decades in the entertainment business, he is still going strong. His love for his work shows. And it is obvious that all of his many fans, not just the ladies, love James Todd Smith.

1968	James Todd Smith is born.
1972	Todd's father shoots his mother and grandfather.
1984	Sends demo tape to Rick Rubin of Def Jam Recordings, which releases "I Need a Break."
1985	Releases first album, *Radio*, with Def Jam; makes cameo appearance in the movie *Krush Groove*.
1986	Appears in the movie *Wildcats*; records song for film's soundtrack.
1987	Meets Simone Johnson, his future wife; releases second album, *Bigger and Deffer*.
1988	Records "Goin' Back to Cali" for the *Less Than Zero* soundtrack.
1989	Son Najee is born; releases third album, *Walking Like A Panther*.
1990	Daughter Italia is born; releases fourth album, *Mama Said Knock You Out*.
1991	Performs on MTV show *Unplugged*; appears in the movie *The Hard Way*.
1992	Wins his first Grammy award for Best Rap Solo Performance.
1993	Releases fifth album, *14 Shots to the Dome*.
1995	Marries Simone Johnson; daughter Samaria is born; releases sixth album, *Mr. Smith*; starts work on television show, *In the House*
1996	Releases his seventh album, *All World: The Greatest Hits*, a compilation of the best-selling singles from his first six albums.
1997	Releases eighth album, *Phenomenon*; publishes autobiography, *I Make My Own Rules*.
1998	Appears in the horror movie *Halloween H2O*.

1999	Appears in movies *Any Given Sunday*, *Deep Blue Sea*, and *In Too Deep*.
2000	Releases ninth album, *G.O.A.T.*
2001	Daughter Nina is born; hosts the American Music Awards.
2002	Releases tenth album, *10*.
2003	Appears in movies *Deliver Us From Eva* and *S.W.A.T.*
2004	Releases eleventh album, *The DEFinition*.
2006	Releases twelfth album, *Todd Smith*; appears in the movie *Last Holiday*; starts Todd Smith clothing line.
2008	Releases thirteenth album, *Exit 13*; starts the LL Cool J Collection clothing line at Sears.
2009	Starts work on television show *NCIS: Los Angeles*
2011	Wins NAACP Image Award for Actor in a Drama Series and repeats in 2012 and 2013.
2013	Releases fourteenth album, *Authentic*.

DISCOGRAPHY

1985	*Radio*	2000	*G.O.A.T.*
1987	*Bigger and Deffer*	2002	*10*
1989	*Walking With a Panther*	2004	*The DEFinition*
1990	*Mama Said Knock You Out*	2006	*Todd Smith*
1993	*14 Shots to the Dome*	2008	*Exit 13*
1995	*Mr. Smith*	2013	*Authentic*
1997	*Phenomenon*		

Find Out More

Baughan, Brian. *LL Cool J* (Hip Hop). Broomall, Pennsylvania: Mason Crest, 2007.

Juzwiak, Rich. *LL Cool J* (Library of Hip-Hop Biographies). New York: Rosen Central, 2005.

LL Cool J and Karen Hunter. *I Make My Own Rules*. New York: St. Martin's Press, 1997.

LL Cool J and Dave Honig. *LL Cool J's Platinum Workout: Sculpt Your Best Body Ever with Hollywood's Fittest Star*. Emmaus, Pennsylvania: Rodale Books, 2010.

Shekell, Dustin. *LL Cool J* (Hip-Hop Stars). New York: Chelsea House, 2007.

Works Consulted

_____. "LL Cool J Eager to Prove Himself on 'NCIS' Spinoff." *Chicago Tribune*, August 3, 2009.

_____. "LL Cool J." *Jet*, September 22, 1997.

_____. "Muhammad Ali Celebrates Birthday," ESPN, February 9, 2012. http://espn.go.com/boxing/story/_/id/7591458/stars-honor-muhammad-ali-70th-birthday-gala-vegas

Beckerman, Jim. "A Cool Transition Rapper LL Cool J Finds Movies A Better Outlet for His Talents Than Music." *Pittsburgh Post-Gazette*, September 2, 1999.

Chappell, Kevin. "After 20 Years in Hip-Hop LL Cool J Comes Clean About Plastic Surgery, Steroid Use, and Heartbreak." *Ebony*, July 2006.

Fields, Tim. "Sears, LL Cool J Launch Clothing Line." *Brandweek*, May 28, 2008.

Guzman, Rafer. "Fast Chat: LL Cool J." *Newsday*, April 23, 2006.

Hoffman, Melody K. "Rap Icon LL Cool J." *Jet*, September 1, 2008.

Holden, Stephen. "From Rock to Rap." *New York Times*, April 26, 1987.

Jacobson, Aileen. "LL Cool J." *Long Island Pulse Magazine*, September 29, 2010.

Jimmy Kimmel Live, April 10, 2012.

LL Cool J's Family Makes Him Tear Up (Video). Huffington Post, http://www.huffingtonpost.com/2013/01/24/ ll-cool-j-family-kids-children-_n_2542253.html

Murray, Sonia. "Q & A/LL Cool J, Rapper: Family-Friendly CD, Sears Clothing Line." *Atlanta Journal*, September 9, 2008.

Shen, Maxine. "Buddy System—O'Donnell and LL Cool J Take 'NCIS' Spin-Off to LA." *New York Post*, September 20, 2009.

Touré. "LL Cool J, 14 Shots to the Dome." *Rolling Stone*, May 13, 1993.

Weisel, Al. "Q&A: LL Cool J." *Rolling Stone*, June 27, 1996.

On the Internet

LL Cool J Biography, Biography.com
http://www.biography.com/people/ll-cool-j-16450351

NCIS: Los Angeles Cast: LL Cool J, CBS.com
http://www.cbs.com/shows/ncis_los_angeles/cast/36191

LL Cool—Internet Movie Database
http://www.imdb.com/name/nm0005112/

LL Cool J—MTV
http://www.mtv.com/artists/ll-cool-j/

LL Cool J—Rolling Stone Artists
http://www.rollingstone.com/music/artists/ll-cool-j

INDEX

DISCARD